BATCHAWANA SILL

BATCHAWANA SILLY STUFF

Emily Hearn

Illustrated by

Gailon Valleau

Hidden Brook Press

First Edition

Hidden Brook Press
www.HiddenBrookPress.com
writers@HiddenBrookPress.com

Batchawana Silly Stuff
by Emily Hearn
Illustrated by Gailon Valleau
Layout and Design – Richard M. Grove

Printed and bound in USA

Library and Archives Canada Cataloguing in Publication

Hearn, Emily, 1925-
    Batchawana silly stuff / Emily Hearn ; illustrated by Gailon Valleau.

A poem.
ISBN 978-1-897475-70-6

    1. Children's poetry, Canadian (English). I. Valleau, Gailon II. Title.

PS8565.E167B38 2011   jC811'.54   C2011-903226-0

Dedicated to
**Morgan and
Siena**

big a wig   tig a wig

Batchawana

Blue

piggy in the 'frigerator

turkey in a shoe

whig a rig   rig a lig
Batchawana

Gray

bees in the dishwasher

lions on a tray

chig a wig   rig a dig
Batchawana

Red

monkeys on the escalator

bison in the bed

rig a dig lig a wig
Batchawana

Yellow

turtles in the percolator

camels on a pillow

fig a wig   sig a lig
Batchawana

Orange

donkeys on the elevator

hippos in the porridge

jig a lig   tig a lig
Batchawana

Green

cows in the humidifier

rabbits on the screen

nig a mig   dig a lig
Batchawana

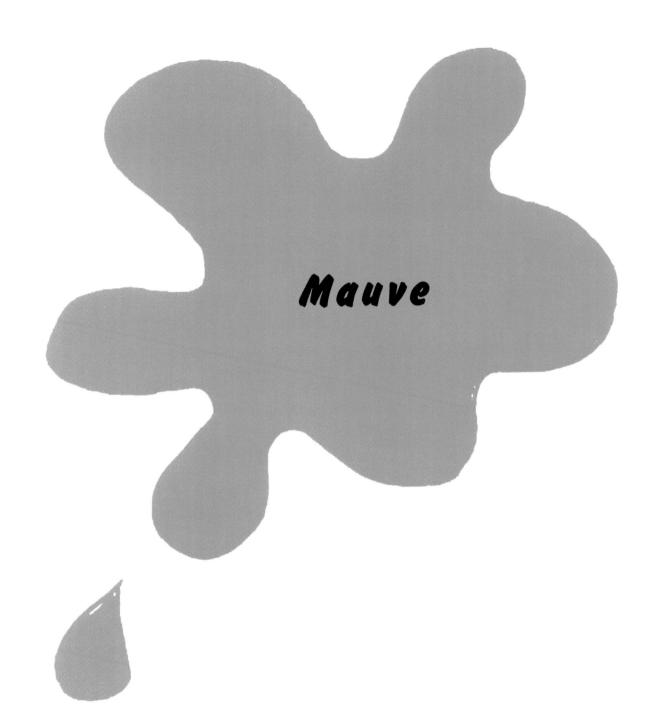

Mauve

crickets on the television

ostrich on the stove

zig a lig   mig a wig
Batchawana

Black

mice on the pencil-sharpener

dragons in the sack

wig a rig   fig a lig
Batchawana

Pink

moose on the radiator

ponies in the sink

gig a lig   nig a dig
Batchawana

Purple

elephants in the laundromat

too many gerbils!

"I hope you had fun with this book. There are ever so many more colours. Maybe you could pick a colour and make up your own rhymes and draw pictures to go with them. I had fun doing that and you can too!"

Emily

Emily Hearn is well known as a children's song and scriptwriter for CBC radio and TVO. An author of children's books, writer with Mark Thurman, artist, of the Mighty Mites Natural History strip for *OWL magazine*, editor of children's readers for Nelson Canada, online mentor of students' creative writing and as a poet of adult books, *Grass of Green Moment* (Pendas) and *They Look Like This to Me* (Hidden Book Press. She is dedicating this book to her youngest grandchildren, Morgan (5) and Siena (2) Hayter.

Gailon Valleau has been a freelance Artist/Illustrator, among other careers, for the past 30 years or so.She has specialized mostly in portraiture and illustrative design and is currently pursuing a career in Graphic design and illustration. She attended The Ontario College of Art from 1977-1980, majoring in Fine Art.

Published books so far include *Song of Three Pirates, Cool Blues* and various other book cover designs.

She has resided in Haliburton, Ont. for the past 25 years.

CPSIA information can be obtained
at www.ICGtesting.com
234712LV00001BA

9781897475706